The Official
Arsenal
Annual 2009

Written By Chas Newkey-Burden

A Grange Publication

© 2008. Published by Grange Communications Ltd.,
Edinburgh, under licence from Arsenal Football Club.
Printed in the EU.

Every effort has been made to ensure the accuracy of
information within this publication but the publishers
cannot be held responsible for any errors or omissions.
Views expressed are those of the author and do not
necessarily represent those of the publishers or the
football club. All rights reserved.

Photographs © Arsenal Football Club.
Arsenal logo and crest are registered trademarks of
The Arsenal Football Club plc.

ISBN 978-1-906211-27-1

£6.99

Contents

Dear Supporters,

Welcome to the Official Arsenal Annual 2009.

I feel very proud of the way our young squad performed during the 2007/08 season, particularly the hard work and commitment they showed. We were all disappointed that these efforts did not lead to us securing a trophy, but I believe that the squad has continued to develop and has shown great character.

There were a number of memorable performances over the season, not least the historic victory over AC Milan at the San Siro. The players stood up to the challenge of fighting for four trophies. They did incredibly well, leading the Premier League for much of the season, and this can only be very exciting for the future.

We are all excited about the 2008/09 season and I am confident that we can challenge again this year. I feel that the squad has all the qualities needed to be successful and I believe that we can compete for all four trophies this campaign.

This Club is special and the team has fantastic spirit and commitment. I feel that these qualities, along with the fantastic support of our fans, will make the 2008/09 season a successful one for Arsenal Football Club.

Thank you for your continued support.

AUGUST

Arsenal kicked off their second season at Emirates Stadium with new faces in the squad and high hopes for a fantastic campaign. Here, we relive the most memorable moments.

The season began with an error and a fightback. In the opening minute of the game against Fulham, an uncharacteristic Jens Lehmann slip gifted the visitors an early lead. However, late goals from Robin van Persie and Alexander Hleb grabbed the Gunners a richly deserved victory.

Van Persie was again on target as Arsenal grabbed a 1-1 draw at Ewood Park. New striker Eduardo made his first start in a match that proved Wenger's team could hold their own in the most physical and tough of games. It was a wet, windy and grey afternoon and the game was a traditional English scrap.

Back at Emirates Stadium, the sun shone as Cesc Fabregas netted a stunning late winner against Manchester City. The Spaniard played a slick one-two with Hleb and fired an unstoppable shot to secure victory. It was the first goal the visitors had conceded all season.

12 August Arsenal 2-1 Fulham (Van Persie 83, Hleb 90)

19 August Blackburn Rovers 1-1 Arsenal (Van Persie 18)

25 August Arsenal 1-0 Manchester City (Fabregas 80)

SEPTEMBER

The first month of the season had been an unbeaten one for Arsenal and the players and management were determined to continue this fine form – they did.

A glorious Premiership month for the Gunners began with a convincing home win against Portsmouth. Emmanuel Adebayor, Tomas Rosicky and Fabregas were on target in the 3-1 victory. Then it was time for the first North London derby of the season. Although Tottenham took the lead at White Hart Lane, a brace from Adebayor and another from in-form Fabregas gave Wenger's team a convincing victory.

Back at Emirates, the boys in red were in even more convincing form against Derby County who they thrashed 5-0. The highlight of the emphatic performance was Adebayor's hat-trick. The other scorers were Abou Diaby and Fabregas.

The trip to West Ham United completed a winning September for the Gunners. It had been seven years since Arsenal had left Upton Park victorious but a headed goal from van Persie in the 13th minute was enough to break that hoodoo. The goal came from a fantastic cross from Alexander Hleb which the Dutchman converted in style. The win put Arsenal three points clear at the top of the Premiership.

2 September Arsenal 3-1 Portsmouth (Adebayor 7, Fabregas 35, Rosicky 59)

15 September Tottenham Hotspur 1-3 Arsenal (Adebayor 66, 90, Fabregas 81)

22 September Arsenal 5-0 Derby County (Diaby 10, Adebayor 25, 50, 80, Fabregas 70)

29 September West Ham United 0-1 Arsenal (Van Persie 13)

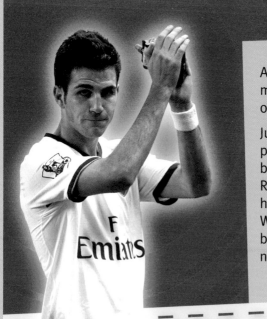

Arsenal remained unbeaten in October and spent much of the month where they belong – at the top of the Premiership.

Just 14 minutes into their clash with newly-promoted Sunderland, Arsenal were 2-0 ahead but that was far from the end of the story. Soon, Roy Keane's men had drawn level and the Gunners had a real match on their hands. Substitute Theo Walcott produced some magical moments, the best of which was when he set up van Persie to net the winner 10 minutes from time.

7 October Arsenal 3-2 Sunderland (Van Persie 7, 81, Senderos 14)

20 October Arsenal 2-0 Bolton Wanderers (Toure 67, Rosicky 81)

28 October Liverpool 1-1 Arsenal (Fabregas 80)

OCTOBER

Arsenal's next win – their 11th consecutive victory – was against Bolton Wanderers. Kolo Toure opened his scoring account for the season with a fine second-half free-kick and the lead was doubled when Rosicky smashed home Walcott's cross with nine minutes left.

Having lost their place at the top of the table, the Gunners travelled to Anfield to face Liverpool. When Steven Gerrard gave the hosts an early lead, Arsenal faced a struggle to get back in the game. However, with 10 minutes left, Fabregas ran onto a Hleb through ball and levelled the score, sending his team back to the Premiership summit.

NOVEMBER

As winter arrived, the Gunners were forced to work extra hard to secure Premiership points. With their captain leading by example, they were once more in fine fettle.

Against Manchester United, William Gallas opened the scoring with an unfortunate own goal, and then netted a late equaliser to keep Arsenal at the top of the Premiership. In between, this breathless match also featured a close-range goal from Cristiano Ronaldo and a fine volley from Fabregas.

Emmanuel Adebayor scored the Club's 1000th in Premiership football as Arsenal beat Reading 3-1 to return to the Premiership summit, having fallen to second since the previous game. It was an impressive performance in Berkshire from the Gunners, with Flamini and Hleb also netting fine strikes.

Back at Emirates, Arsenal faced an amazingly resilient Wigan Athletic. For 84 largely frustrating minutes, the hosts fought in vain to break down their visitors' defences. But cometh the hour, cometh the man and captain Gallas headed home a Sagna cross to put the Gunners ahead. 120 seconds later Rosicky converted a Bendtner cross to confirm the win.

3 November Arsenal 2-2 Manchester United (Fabregas 48, Gallas 90)

12 November Reading 1-3 Arsenal (Flamini 44, Adebayor 52, Hleb 78)

24 November Arsenal 2-0 Wigan Athletic (Gallas 84, Rosicky 86)

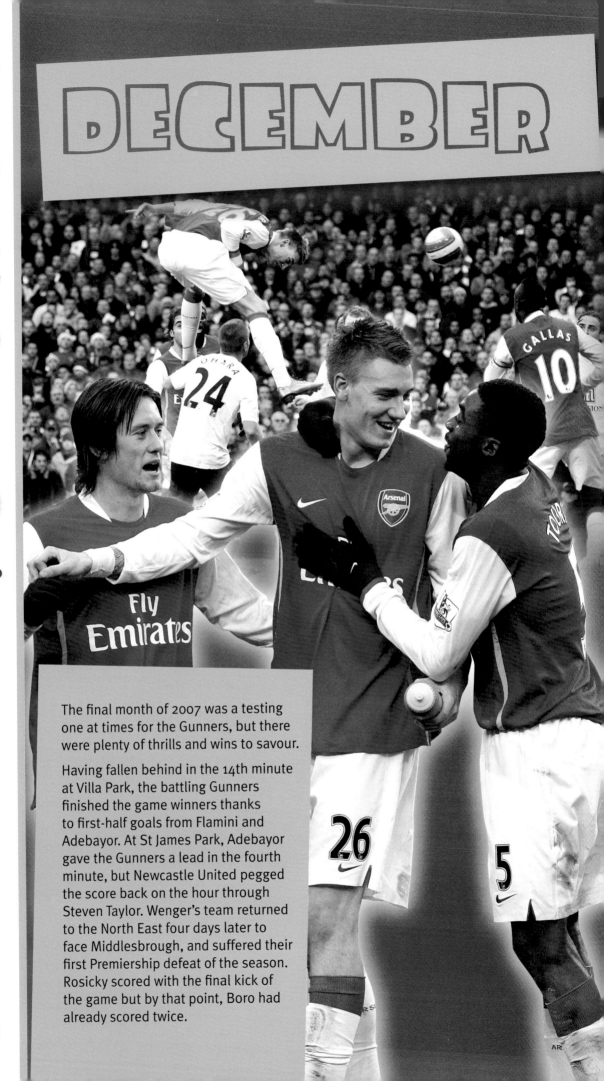

DECEMBER

The final month of 2007 was a testing one at times for the Gunners, but there were plenty of thrills and wins to savour.

Having fallen behind in the 14th minute at Villa Park, the battling Gunners finished the game winners thanks to first-half goals from Flamini and Adebayor. At St James Park, Adebayor gave the Gunners a lead in the fourth minute, but Newcastle United pegged the score back on the hour through Steven Taylor. Wenger's team returned to the North East four days later to face Middlesbrough, and suffered their first Premiership defeat of the season. Rosicky scored with the final kick of the game but by that point, Boro had already scored twice.

However, the Gunners returned to the top of the league with a 1-0 victory over Chelsea, with Gallas scoring the winner against his former team. Then came a frantic North London derby. Adebayor opened the scoring three minutes into the second half but the Gunners were pegged back in the 66th minute. Tottenham nearly took the lead when they were awarded a penalty but Manuel Almunia bravely turned it aside.

Enter substitute Nicklas Bendtner who scored the winner with his first touch.

After a goalless draw at Portsmouth, the Gunners travelled to Everton where they went behind after 20 minutes. However, in the second half they fought back with a brace from Eduardo, his first Premiership goals. Adebayor and Rosicky added their own goals. A wonderful win to cap a fine month!

1 December Aston Villa 1-2 Arsenal (Flamini 24, Adebayor 36)

5 December Newcastle United 1-1 (Adebayor 4)

9 December Middlesbrough 2-1 Arsenal (Rosicky 90)

16 December Arsenal 1-0 Chelsea (Gallas 45)

22 December Arsenal 2-1 Tottenham Hotspur (Adebayor 48, Bendtner 75)

26 December Portsmouth 0-0 Arsenal

29 December Everton 1-4 Arsenal (Eduardo 47, 58, Adebayor 78, Rosicky 90)

JANUARY

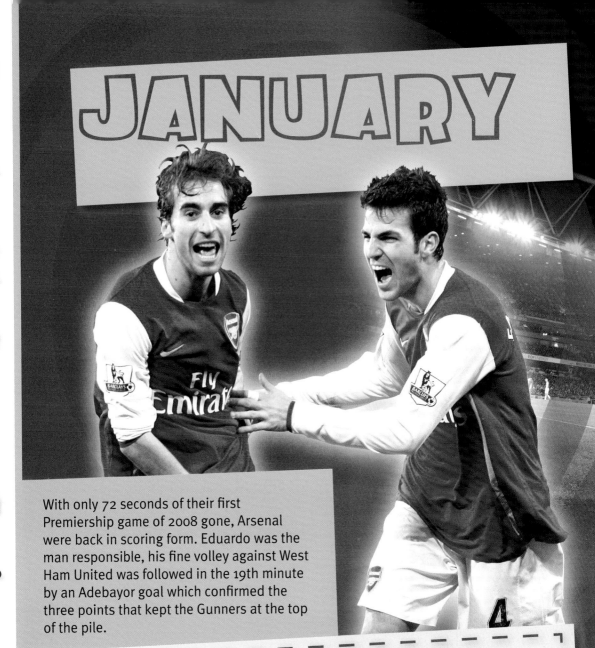

With only 72 seconds of their first Premiership game of 2008 gone, Arsenal were back in scoring form. Eduardo was the man responsible, his fine volley against West Ham United was followed in the 19th minute by an Adebayor goal which confirmed the three points that kept the Gunners at the top of the pile.

1 January Arsenal 2-0 West Ham United (Eduardo 2, Adebayor 19)

12 January Arsenal 1-1 Birmingham City (Adebayor 22)

19 January Fulham 0-3 Arsenal (Adebayor 20, 39, Rosicky 82)

29 January Arsenal 3-0 Newcastle United (Adebayor 40, Flamini 73, Fabregas 80)

The Togolese hitman was again on target at Birmingham City, but the visitors drew level three minutes into the second-half. The two dropped points meant Arsenal lost vital ground in the title race. At Fulham, Adebayor netted his 14th and 15th goals of the season as Arsenal cruised to a 3-0 victory.

Back at Emirates, the highlight of Arsenal's 3-0 romp over Newcastle was Flamini's 30 yard thunderbolt. Either side of his wonder strike Adebayor and Fabregas had also netted against Kevin Keegan's men.

FEBRUARY

February began well for Arsenal, but was to end with a distressing afternoon in the Midlands.

The versatile brilliance of Adebayor was confirmed once more at Manchester City, where he scored twice and also turned provider. He converted a Sagna cross and a Hleb cutback, and in between those strikes he set up Eduardo. 3-1 to the Arsenal, and a return to the top of the table for Wenger's wonderlads.

At Ewood Park, Arsenal went five points clear thanks to a 2-0 victory. Senderos gave the Gunners the lead in the fourth minute, but it was only in the 90th minute when Adebayor doubled the lead that the visitors could relax during a challenging evening.

However, perhaps the toughest game of the season came at Birmingham City. Eduardo broke his leg in the third minute and the horror of his injury overshadowed the rest of the game. Theo Walcott netted his first two Premiership strikes but the Gunners were pegged back to a draw due to a late Birmingham City penalty.

2 February Manchester City 1-3 Arsenal (Adebayor 9, 88, Eduardo 26)

11 February Arsenal 2-0 Blackburn Rovers (Senderos 4, Adebayor 90)

23 February Birmingham City 2-2 Arsenal (Walcott 50, 55)

MARCH

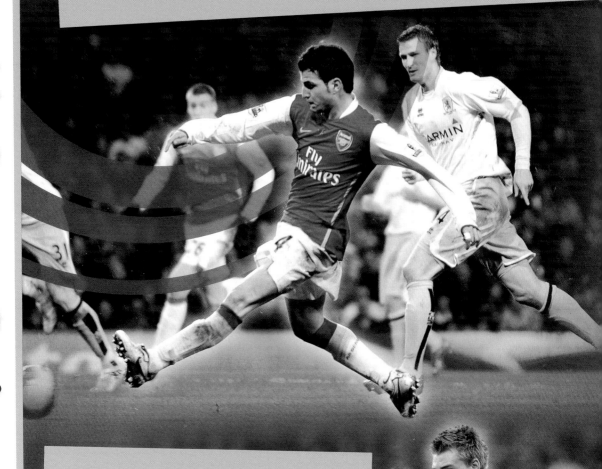

March was certainly a testing month for Arsenal – though it ended in ecstasy.

Arsenal were close to losing their spot at the top of the Premiership when they trailed against Aston Villa at the beginning of the month. However, the team continued to press and press until finally, in injury time, Adebayor nodded down and Bendtner stabbed home from close range.

The points were shared too, when the Gunners travelled to Wigan Athletic. Chris Kirkland saved spectacularly from Adebayor in the opening minute, and from Fabregas in the final minute. In between, the visitors peppered his goal with chances but were unable to break the deadlock.

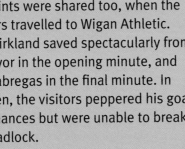

Middlesbrough then arrived at Emirates and former Gunner Jeremie Aliadiere gave them a first-half lead. With Arsenal staring defeat in the face, Kolo Toure equalised with four minutes left. Once again, the game ended all-square. The following week at Stamford Bridge, Bacary Sagna's first goal for the Club was not enough to avoid defeat by Chelsea.

A testing month ended on the highest of highs as 10-man Arsenal came back from 2-0 down at Bolton Wanderers to win 3-2. Second-half goals from Gallas and van Persie set up a grandstand finish. An own goal from Jlloyd Samuel gave the Gunners a thumping victory and sent the visiting fans into a frenzy.

1 March Arsenal 1-1 Aston Villa (Bendtner 90)

9 March Wigan Athletic 0-0 Arsenal

15 March Arsenal 1-1 Middlesbrough (Toure 86)

23 March Chelsea 2-1 Arsenal (Sagna 58)

29 March Bolton Wanderers 2-3 (Gallas 63, Van Persie 69, Samuel (og) 90)

APRIL

Liverpool were the first opponents of April for Arsène Wenger's men and this Premiership tie was sandwiched between two Champions League clashes with the Merseysiders. Here, Peter Crouch gave the visitors a first-half lead and Bendtner equalised in the second-half.

Next up in a tricky month of fixtures was a trip to Old Trafford. Adebayor opened the scoring but second-half strikes from Ronaldo and Owen Hargreaves claimed the points for United and effectively ended Arsenal's Premiership hopes.

The Togolese striker was again on target against Reading, back at Emirates. Gilberto also scored and it proved to be a comfortable victory against the relegation-threatened Berkshire side.

Where that win was comfortable, the victory over Derby County was simply spectacular. Three second-half goals from Adebayor – his second hat-trick of the season against the Rams – was the pick of the action in a resounding 6-2 victory.

5 April Arsenal 1-1 Liverpool (Bendtner 54)

13 April Manchester United 2-1 Arsenal (Adebayor 48)

19 April Arsenal 2-0 Reading (Adebayor 30, Gilberto 38)

28 April Derby County 2-6 Arsenal (Bendtner 25, Van Persie 39, Adebayor 59, 80, 90, Walcott 78)

MAY

4 May Arsenal 1-0 Everton (Bendtner 77)

11 May Sunderland 0-1 Arsenal (Walcott 24)

Out of the title race, could Arsène Wenger's team nevertheless complete the season in style? They could...

The Gunners completed an unbeaten home campaign for only the second time in their history when they beat Everton 1-0. With 13 minutes remaining, the hosts confirmed their superiority when Bendtner thumped home a header. Also noticeable in this tie was the final bow of goalkeeper Jens Lehmann, who was cheered to the rafters as he made his final appearance for the Club.

The season was concluded at the Stadium Of Light. Theo Walcott shone brightest on the day and his winning goal was richly deserved. It had been a season of highs and lows for Arsenal, but it ended on a high with three points and a third-place finish.

CASE FOR THE DEFENCE

All members of the Arsenal defence have certain things in common: they are solid, speedy and skilful. However, they all have different backgrounds, strengths and stories. Here, we take a look at their journey so far...

GAEL CLICHY

Date of birth: July 26, 1985

Previous club: Cannes

The knowledge: Gael became the youngest player to win a Premiership winners' medal in 2004 at the age of 18. He then suffered from a series of injury problems but has since put those woes behind him to become the Premiership's most revered left-back. He was voted into the PFA Team of the Year for the 2007/08 season.

Random fact: Gael was a key member of the 'Invincible' side that went 49 matches unbeaten.

WILLIAM GALLAS

Date of birth: August 17, 1977

Previous clubs: Caen, Marseille, Chelsea

The knowledge: Versatile William can play at left-back when needed but it is in the heart of the defence where he performs most memorably. He has an impressive spring, which he uses to prevent goals at the Arsenal end, and score them at the opponents' end. He is a true rock and a formidable opponent. He won the Premiership twice at Chelsea and hopes to repeat that feat with the Gunners.

Random fact: Skipper William was born on the same day as former Club captain Thierry Henry!

JUSTIN HOYTE

Date of birth: November 20, 1984

Previous club: None

The Knowledge: Londoner Justin is a solid, pacey and adventurous defender. His style of play was summed up by his debut goal against Charlton. He began the move in defence, sprinted forward and finished the move with a fine goal. Adaptable and determined, Justin is a fantastic player with a bright future.

Random Fact: Justin made his Gunners debut against Southampton in May 2003 – the first game of the record-breaking 49-match unbeaten run.

BACARY SAGNA

Date of birth: February 14, 1983

Previous club: Auxerre

The knowledge: A powerful and consistent performer, Bacary enjoys belting forward into the attack as well as defending like a lion. He made his debut in August 2007 and by the end of the season he had become a household name and was, along with his full-back partner Gael, named in the PFA Team of the Year for the season. Even better things are surely to come from this remarkable performer.

Random fact: Bacary's cousin Ibrahima has played in the Premiership with Reading FC.

PHILIPPE SENDEROS

Date of birth: February 14, 1985

Previous club: Servette

The Knowledge: Making his debut a year after he signed for the Club, Swiss man Philippe quickly impressed in a red shirt, not least in the 2005 FA Cup Final against Manchester United where his performance helped the Gunners to victory. He has since become a star player on the European stage too, and for his national side of Switzerland.

Random Fact: Because his birthday is on Valentine's Day, Philippe has been known to receive two sets of greetings cards on his big day!

KOLO TOURE

Date of birth: March 19, 1981

Previous club: ASEC Mimosas

The knowledge: It was during the unbeaten league campaign of 2003/04 that Kolo cemented his place in Arsenal history. He missed just one league match that season and became a firm favourite. He has since transformed himself from promising youngster to a seasoned performer who helps guide his younger team-mates on and off the field. His great timing and positional awareness make him an immense asset.

Random fact: Kolo has two younger brothers who play professional football. They are called Yaya and Ibrahim.

QUALIFYING ROUND

Sparta Prague v Arsenal

The Czechs dominated the first-half of the match but in the second-half, fine goals from Fabregas and Hleb allowed the Gunners to take control of the tie. The pick of the pair was the Spaniard's strike, which was created by a fine run and pass from Clichy. Advantage Arsenal.

Euro fact: This was Arsenal's third victory at this stadium in the past seven years.

Arsenal v Sparta Prague

This was a comfortable victory for Arsène Wenger's team. Just seven minutes in, Rosicky made it 1-0 on the night and 3-0 on aggregate, effectively ending the contest. From then on, the home side effortlessly bossed proceedings. In the final 10 minutes, both Fabregas and Eduardo scored. The North Londoners were through to the group stage!

Euro fact: Eduardo's goal was his first for the Gunners.

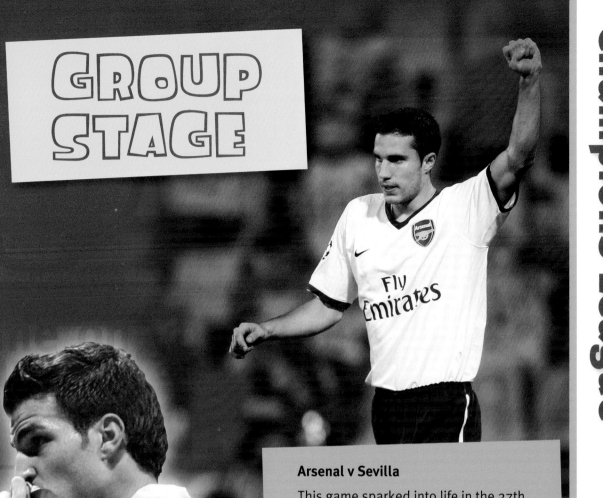

GROUP STAGE

Champions League

Arsenal v Sevilla

This game sparked into life in the 27th minute when a deflected Fabregas shot opened the scoring. In the second-half, van Persie and Eduardo joined the midfield ace on the scoresheet. Van Persie's was a close range shot, and Eduardo's was a simple effort at the end of a typically flowing Arsenal move. This tie between two of Europe's most fluent sides was deservedly won by the Gunners.

Euro fact: The then Sevilla boss Juande Ramos now manages Arsenal's rivals Tottenham Hotspur.

Steaua Bucharest v Arsenal

This was a tie in which patience and persistence would be rewarded. For Arsenal, that reward came after 76 minutes when Dutchman van Persie fired home a cutback from Adebayor. It had been a tough and somewhat frantic game up until this point, with an Arsenal 'goal' disallowed in the first half. Having taken the lead, Arsenal protected it vigorously and claimed another three points in their Champions League campaign.

Euro fact: This was Arsenal's ninth straight win.

15 August 2007 Sparta Prague 0-2 Arsenal (Fabregas 72, Hleb 90)

29 August 2007 Arsenal 3-0 Sparta Prague (Rosicky 7, Fabregas 82, Eduardo 89)

19 September 2007 Arsenal 3-0 Sevilla (Fabregas 27, Van Persie 59, Eduardo 90)

21

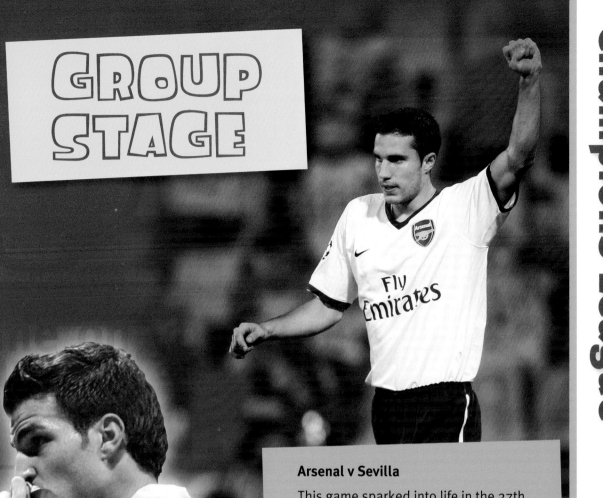

GROUP STAGE

Arsenal v Slavia Prague

What a night of football. The highlights of this romp were the two goals scored by Walcott and Fabregas. Indeed, the Englishman was only prevented from scoring a hat-trick by a stupendous save from the visitors' goalkeeper. Hleb and Bentdner also netted on the night, and the scoreline was completed by a Slavia own goal. The Gunners were every bit as brilliant as the final score suggests. This tie really made Europe sit up and take notice of the emerging excellence of the young Gunners.

Euro fact: The only other time the Gunners have won 7-0 in Europe was in 1993, against Standard Liege.

Slavia Prague v Arsenal

After the joyful seven-goal win over Slavia at Emirates Stadium, the Gunners drew a blank here on a wet and windy evening. Mr Wenger had made eight changes since the previous game and the side failed to click. Neither did they register a scoring chance worthy of that name. However, this result guaranteed Arsenal a place in the knockout stages, so nobody was complaining.

Euro fact: This was the 100th Champions League tie that Arsène Wenger had taken control of, excluding qualifying games.

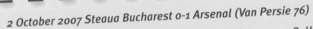

GROUP STAGE

2 October 2007 Steaua Bucharest 0-1 Arsenal (Van Persie 76)

23 October 2007 Arsenal 7-0 Slavia Prague (Fabregas 5, 58, Huback (og) 25, Walcott 54, 55, Hleb 50, Bendtner 88)

7 November 2007 Slavia Prague 0-0 Arsenal

27 November 2007 Sevilla 3-1 Arsenal (Eduardo 11)

12 December 2007 Arsenal 2-1 Steaua Bucharest (Diaby 8, Bendtner 42)

Sevilla v Arsenal

In the 11th minute, Arsenal took the lead when Eboue released Bendtner who crossed for Eduardo to nod home at the far post. The Croatian had done well to score, for he was under great pressure from his opponents. That goal proved to be the highpoint for Arsenal on a tough night of football. They conceded three goals and this result knocked them off their perch at the top of Group H. Could they bounce back in the final group match?

Euro fact: **This result brought to an end a 28-match unbeaten run for the Gunners.**

Arsenal v Steaua Bucharest

Yes they could, though they would have to settle for second place in the final Group H standings. Goals from Abou Diaby and Bendtner were enough to secure victory for Arsenal, with Zaharia's strike a mere consolation for the visitors. However, results elsewhere meant that Arsenal were pipped to the post for top place by Sevilla. Nonetheless, the most important fact was that Arsenal had comfortably qualified for the knockout stages.

Euro fact: **All seven of Arsenal's substitutes were capped international players.**

Team	P	W	D	L	F	A	GD	Pts
Sevilla	6	5	0	1	14	7	+7	15
Arsenal	6	4	1	1	14	4	+10	13
Slavia Prague	6	1	2	3	5	16	-11	5
Steaua Bucharest	6	0	1	5	4	10	-6	1

Champions League

23

KNOCKOUT STAGES

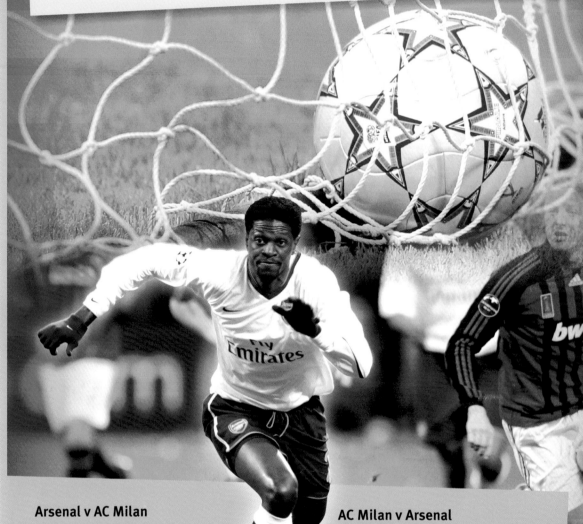

Arsenal v AC Milan

The first-leg of this knockout tie was as cagey and tight as one might expect of such a high-stakes encounter involving an Italian side. Eduardo, Eboue and Adebayor all had chances to open the scoring in the second-half, but the Gunners were unable to breach a resolute AC Milan defence. The Togolese's chance was the closest: his header rattled the bar in the final minute. This set up an absolutely tantalising prospect for the second-leg, a match that didn't disappoint.

Euro fact: Six players returned from injury for this tie.

AC Milan v Arsenal

Arsenal sailed into the quarter-finals with a magnificent performance against the holders AC Milan. In the 84th minute, the majestic Fabregas let fly from 30 yards and joy ensued among the visiting fans as they watched his strike fly into the back of the net. The celebrations on and off the pitch were wild. Understandably, that set up some tense closing minutes, but the visitors could afford to draw breath when Adebayor converted Walcott's excellent cross. What a fantastic evening.

Euro fact: This was the first time an English side had won at the San Siro against AC Milan.

QUARTER FINALS

Arsenal v Liverpool

Arsenal grabbed the lead in the 23rd minute, when Adebayor fired home a powerful header. However, that lead lasted just 120 seconds and Dirk Kuyt was the visitor responsible for equalling the scoreline. During the second-half, Arsenal had a strong claim for a penalty and Fabregas came close to claiming a winner from open play. However, while the scoreline remained 1-1, Liverpool effectively had the advantage going into the second leg.

Euro fact: Adebayor's goal was his 24th of the season.

Liverpool v Arsenal

For the neutral, this must have been an entertaining night. For Liverpool fans, it will have been an ecstatic evening. For Arsenal, it was eventful but heartbreaking. The Gunners took a deserved lead after 13 minutes through Diaby. After two Liverpool goals, Adebayor scored in the 84th minute and thanks to the away goals rule, the Gunners were minutes from the semi-finals. Then, two late Liverpool goals knocked the visitors out. It was a disappointing end to a promising and entertaining Champions League campaign for the Club.

20 February 2008 Arsenal 0-0 AC Milan

4 March 2008 Arsenal 2-0 AC Milan (Fabregas 84, Adebayor 90)

2 April 2008 Arsenal 1-1 Liverpool (Adebayor 24)

8 April 2008 Liverpool 4-2 Arsenal (Diaby 13, Adebayor 84)

CLASSIC EUROPEAN NIGHTS

Arsenal's 2-0 victory against AC Milan will quite rightly go down in the history books as a special evening in the Club's history. It will take its place alongside many other magnificent Champions League performances that Arsenal have been involved in during recent years. Here, then, is a selection of those classic European nights...

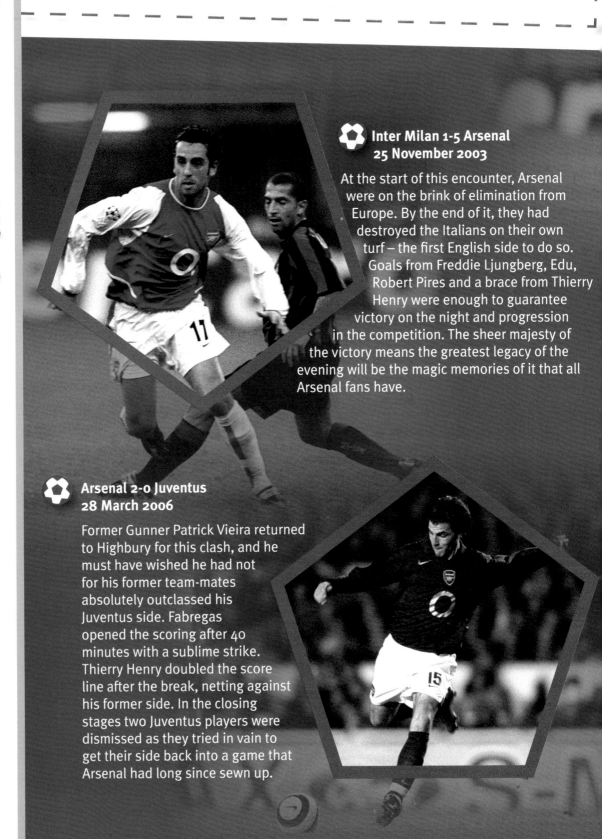

Inter Milan 1-5 Arsenal
25 November 2003

At the start of this encounter, Arsenal were on the brink of elimination from Europe. By the end of it, they had destroyed the Italians on their own turf – the first English side to do so. Goals from Freddie Ljungberg, Edu, Robert Pires and a brace from Thierry Henry were enough to guarantee victory on the night and progression in the competition. The sheer majesty of the victory means the greatest legacy of the evening will be the magic memories of it that all Arsenal fans have.

Arsenal 2-0 Juventus
28 March 2006

Former Gunner Patrick Vieira returned to Highbury for this clash, and he must have wished he had not for his former team-mates absolutely outclassed his Juventus side. Fabregas opened the scoring after 40 minutes with a sublime strike. Thierry Henry doubled the score line after the break, netting against his former side. In the closing stages two Juventus players were dismissed as they tried in vain to get their side back into a game that Arsenal had long since sewn up.

Real Madrid 0-1 Arsenal
21 February 2006

Arsenal absolutely silenced the Bernabeu Stadium with this memorable performance and victory. The visitors dominated the first-half and then two minutes into the second period, their dominance was confirmed numerically when Henry scored a magnificent goal. It proved to be the winner, because Arsenal fought hard to protect their lead. This was the first time that Real Madrid had been beaten at home by an English side in Europe. Well done, Gunners.

Sparta Prague 0-2 Arsenal
15 October 2005

This tie was memorable because it was the one that saw Thierry Henry become the Club's record goalscorer. Eight years and 35 days earlier, Ian Wright had claimed that honour but his record was surpassed by the Frenchman here. The goal itself was fairly everyday, he swivelled, he shot, he scored. However, it made Henry the Club's top scorer of all time. How long will it be until his record is broken? Will it ever be?

Celta Vigo 2-3 Arsenal
24 February 2004

This was Arsenal's first victory in Spain in the Champions League and it was achieved in some style! Edu scored twice and Robert Pires grabbed the winner after Celta had fought their way back into the game. Pires's strike was the pick of the bunch, coming as it did after some fine interplay between him and his fellow Frenchman Thierry Henry. It had been an enthralling encounter, not least as Celta bounced back from their early setback. However, the Gunners emerged triumphant.

WHAT THEY SAID

During any season there are highs and lows, victories and defeats. There are also plenty of interviews. So here is the story of the 2007/08 season told through the words of the men who matter most: the players and management of Arsenal. Goals, victories, tears, hospitals, allergies and dolphins, they're all here.

"Now he can't stop scoring when before he could not. That shows the importance of what goes on in your head."

Arsène Wenger on Cesc Fabregas's goal-fest during 2007/08 season

"No it wasn't perfect. OK it is if you look at the result but I watched it again and you can see we missed some passes and some balls. No game is perfect but some of our goals were that night."

Arsène Wenger following the 7-0 demolition of Slavia Prague in the Champions League

"During the Liverpool game I was getting small patches on my arms, like a stress allergy. I was going crazy!"

Bacary Sagna on watching from the sidelines

"He came here without a CV but he has made a name for himself, which is not easy at a big club."

The manager is impressed with Manuel Almunia's fine form between the sticks

"I would like to thank the medical team here at Arsenal for their efforts as well as the staff at Selly Oak Hospital who carried out the operation on Saturday night. I would also like to say how touched I am by the many messages of support I have received and to be surrounded by my loved ones at this time."

Eduardo is full of gratitude following his leg break against Birmingham City

"I'd like to be a dolphin. I was fortunate to swim with dolphins in America and I love the way they move in the water and jump as high as they can."

Justin Hoyte, when asked what type of animal he'd like to be.

"We don't have to be ashamed of our season. We have given everything we had, it was not our time but we have learnt a lot this season."

Emmanuel Eboue in positive mood, at the end of a tough campaign

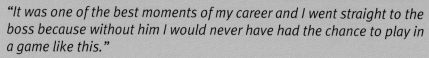

"Perhaps the players will not be so pleased with me because I always like to play in short sleeves, even in the winter. If you are cold it makes you run more!"

As the cold season approaches, captain William Gallas isn't about to wrap up!

"It was one of the best moments of my career and I went straight to the boss because without him I would never have had the chance to play in a game like this."

Cesc Fabregas on his wonder goal at the San Siro against AC Milan

"On Mother's Day I totally forgot to get my Mum something! My brother remembered but I got her some nice perfume later to make up for it!"

Theo Walcott comes clean in his diary

"I had one or two tears in my eyes. It was a great farewell for me. This farewell will always stay in my heart."

Jens Lehmann on his final match for the Gunners

Gael Clichy

FA CUP

Arsenal's FA Cup campaign was the setting for some strong performances, memorable goals and admirable victories. Although the team did not make it beyond the Fifth Round, there was much to enjoy in the cup that cheers.

THIRD ROUND

Away v Burnley

Croatian striker Eduardo opened the scoring at Turf Moor with a cool finish in the ninth minute. It was his sixth goal in his previous four starts for Arsenal. Burnley put up brave resistance but on the hour were reduced to 10 men when Kyle Lafferty was dismissed. With a quarter of an hour remaining, Arsenal's victory was put beyond doubt when Bendtner sailed past the keeper and slotted the ball home.

Match Fact: This was the final match Emmanuel Eboue and Kolo Toure played before leaving for the Africa Cup Of Nations.

FOURTH ROUND

Home v Newcastle United

This was a tighter game than the scoreline suggests. It was only when Adebayor opened the scoring five minutes into the second half that the Gunners began to show their full class. The Togolese striker added a second on 84 minutes and then a Fabregas free-kick was accidentally guided into the net by Nicky Butt. The Gunners were through to the Fifth Round!

Match Fact: This was the first away match Newcastle United played after manager Kevin Keegan's return to the club.

FIFTH ROUND

Away v Manchester United

Just 20 minutes into this tie, Arsenal were already two goals behind thanks to strikes from Fletcher and Rooney. Nani made it three before half-time. The Gunners were reduced to 10 men when Eboue was dismissed and their misery was compounded when Fletcher made it 4-0 to United in the 74th minute. It had been a disappointing match for the injury-hit Arsenal side.

Match Fact: Wenger was without nine first-team players for this tie, and of those players who travelled to Manchester, three were carrying injuries.

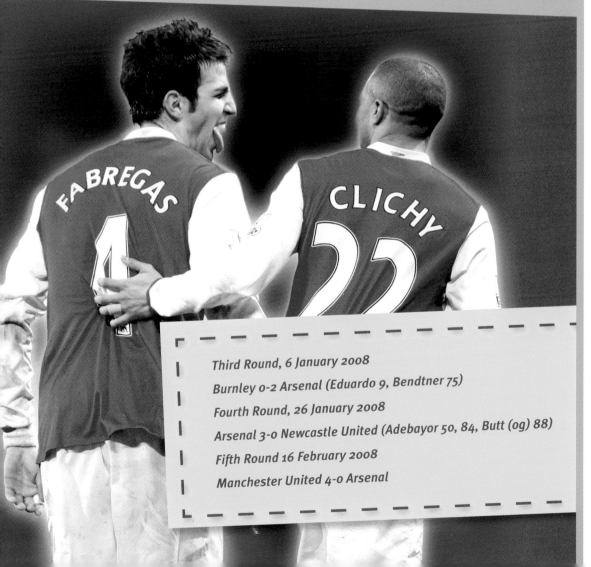

Third Round, 6 January 2008

Burnley 0-2 Arsenal (Eduardo 9, Bendtner 75)

Fourth Round, 26 January 2008

Arsenal 3-0 Newcastle United (Adebayor 50, 84, Butt (og) 88)

Fifth Round 16 February 2008

Manchester United 4-0 Arsenal

MIDDLE CLASS

They pull the strings in the midfield as they patrol the central pastures of the Emirates Stadium pitch. But how much do you know about the Arsenal midfielders?

DENILSON

Date of birth: February 16, 1988

Previous Club: São Paulo

The knowledge: Brazilian Denilson looks set to emerge into even more regular first-team reckoning in the near future. Soon after he arrived in England he was dubbed "the next Cesc Fabregas". Mr Wenger, meanwhile, described him as "a little bit in between Tomás Rosicky and Gilberto". Far from feeling pressurised by this, he simply continued to do what he does best – star in the midfield. Quick, nimble and with a fine eye for a pass or a goal, he is a fantastic prospect and will be terrorising opponents across Europe very soon.

Random Fact: His full name is Denilson Pereira Neves.

ABOU DIABY

Date of birth: May 11, 1986

Previous Club: Auxerre

The knowledge: Powerful, tall and courageous, Diaby is the consummate modern midfielder. After picking up a serious injury early in his Gunner career, he has since bounced back to first-team excellence. The man who progressed through the same Auxerre youth academy as Eric Cantona has risen to the big stage with grace. His goal at Anfield in the Champions League quarter-final proved he can cut it in the highest of high pressure games. Abou is set to become a Gunners legend.

Random Fact: Abou has often been compared to former Gunners midfield ace Patrick Vieira.

CESC FABREGAS

Date of birth: May 4, 1987

Previous Club: Barcelona

The knowledge: Having become the Club's youngster ever player and goal-scorer, Cesc is now perhaps the greatest player in his position in the world. The young Spaniard is crisp in the tackle, incisive in passing and increasingly deadly in front of goal. He was the PFA Team Player of the Year for 2007/08, and was named in the PFA Player of the Year for the same campaign.

Random fact: One of Cesc's favourite television programmes is US drama Desperate Housewives.

AARON RAMSEY

Date of birth: December 26, 1990

Previous Club: Cardiff City

The knowledge: Young ace Aaron has represented Wales at Under-21 level and became the youngest player ever to represent his country at this level in August 2007, in a 4-3 victory over the Sweden Under-21s. He was the youngest ever player to represent Cardiff City, with his substitute appearance against Hull City on April 28, 2007, at just 16 years 124 days. He had already scored at Emirates Stadium before his move to the Club, in an FA Youth Cup quarter-final match in February 2007.

Random Fact: Aaron was a substitute for Cardiff City in the 2008 FA Cup Final against Portsmouth at Wembley Stadium.

TOMAS ROSICKY

Date of birth: October 4, 1980

Previous Clubs: Sparta Prague, Borussia Dortmund

The knowledge: Skilful and fast, the Czech ace has become a firm favourite of the Arsenal fans. With his accurate, intelligent passing and his fine eye for goal, he has acquired the nickname 'Little Mozart'. This is a fitting nickname as he orchestrates much of what is brilliant in the Arsenal midfield. By the age of 25, he had already represented the Czech Republic in three major tournaments and won league titles in two countries. He hopes to make that three soon.

Random Fact: Tomas's brother Jirí has played for a host of clubs including Sparta Prague and Atletico Madrid.

SAMIR NASRI

Date of birth: June 26, 1987

Previous Club: Marseille

The knowledge: Samir is an attacking midfielder with fantastic pace and skill. He was voted as the French Ligue 1 'Young Player of the Year' for 2006/07 and was also Olympique Marseille's Player of the Year for 2007. The French international won the UEFA Intertoto Cup in 2005, and was a French Cup runner-up in 2006 and 2007. In his final season at Marseille, he helped his side secure Champions League qualification.

Random Fact: Samir's grandparents moved to France from Algeria.

ARSENAL 2007/08 TRIVIA

Want the story of the 2007/08 season in numbers? Then you've come to the right page. Here, you will find every stat and fact about the campaign that you could ever wish for. From hawks to goals, this is the definitive guide to a memorable year for the Gunners.

Arsenal moved **2** places up the fair play table. **2**

1st Emmanuel Adebayor's goal at the San Siro was his **1st** Champions League goal for the Gunners.

27

Arsenal kept **27** clean sheets during the **58** games they contested during the 2007/08 season. Good going, lads!

26 **58**

36 In 2006/07 the Club accumulated **26** points on their travels, **16** worse than champions Manchester United. In 2007/08 they earned **36**, one more than the fierce rivals. **16**

12 different nationalities scored for Arsenal in the Premier League during the 2007/08 season. **12**

AC Milan had played **11** matches against English opposition at the San Siro without defeat prior to Arsenal beating them there in March 2008.

1st **50th**

Both the **1st**, and **50th**, games at Emirates Stadium were against Aston Villa and ended in **1-1** draws.

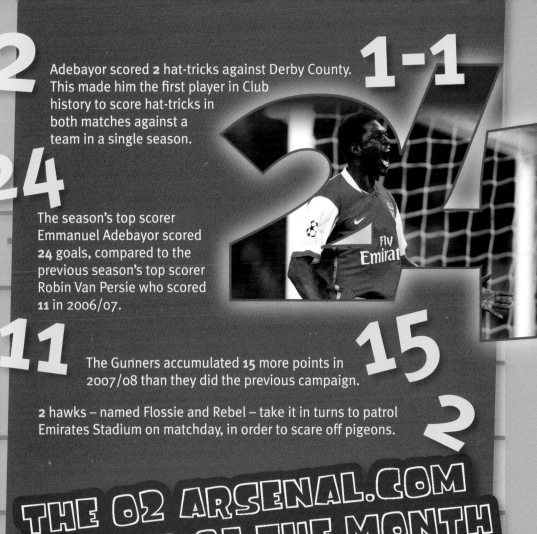

2

Adebayor scored **2** hat-tricks against Derby County. This made him the first player in Club history to score hat-tricks in both matches against a team in a single season.

1-1

24

The season's top scorer Emmanuel Adebayor scored **24** goals, compared to the previous season's top scorer Robin Van Persie who scored **11** in 2006/07.

11

15

The Gunners accumulated **15** more points in 2007/08 than they did the previous campaign.

2 hawks – named Flossie and Rebel – take it in turns to patrol Emirates Stadium on matchday, in order to scare off pigeons.

2

THE O2 ARSENAL.COM PLAYER OF THE MONTH

August – Cesc Fabregas
September - Cesc Fabregas
October - Cesc Fabregas
November – William Gallas
December – Eduardo

January – Emmanuel Adebayor
February – Eduardo
March – Cesc Fabregas
April – Theo Walcott

723   475   817   17   2

Cesc Fabregas was named PFA Young Player of the Season for 2007/08.

5   61

Arsenal was voted best 'Overall Club Experience' in a poll of Premier League fans.

YOUNG GUNS GO FOR IT!

Last year, Arsenal went all the way to the Final of the Carling Cup with a youthful line-up. This time, the Gunners were aiming to go one better and win the trophy. They came very close...

Home v Newcastle United

Arsenal began their Carling Cup campaign with a majestic performance in which the young line-up dominated their more experienced opponents and richly deserved their victory. Only Theo Walcott and Philippe Senderos retained their places from the side that contested the Club's previous Premiership clash, the remainder of the side were mostly drawn from the second string.

However, in the second-half particularly the team played like seasoned veterans. With eight minutes left, Armand Traore crossed from the left and Bendtner sent a poweful header past Shay Given. Minutes later, Diaby set up Denilson for a cracking second in to the top corner. A fantastic start to the campaign, which boded very well indeed.

Away v Sheffield United

The Gunners stormed into the final eight of the competition with a cracking win at Bramall Lane. Such was the youthfulness of this Arsenal line-up that the bench contained a player as young as 16 in the shape of Henri Lansbury. Yet again, the team played like men much older than their collective years.

Eduardo scored in the eighth minute with a long-distance strike. Then, five minutes after half-time he ran onto a pass from Kieran Gibbs to double the visitors' lead. Then Brazilian ace Denilson fired home midway through the second period and the Gunners victory was safe. The home crowd clapped the Gunners off at the end of a match that they had dominated – and won in style.

Away v Blackburn Rovers

This match was full of drama: five goals, a dismissal, extra-time and a last-minute winner. Phew. In the first-half, the Gunners had taken a deserved two-goal lead through midfielder Diaby and hotshot Eduardo. Santa Cruz scored either side of the break to draw the home side level.

Then, Arsenal lost Denilson to a red card and suddenly the stage seemed set for Rovers to push on to victory. Not so fast! Alex Song surged forward from the defence and set up Eduardo who fired home a late winner, after the tie had gone to extra-time. A spectacular, memorable evening of football ending in victory for Arsenal.

Home v Tottenham Hotspur

Going into this game, Arsène Wenger's team had avoided defeat at the hands of their rivals for 20 games. For much of the game, the chances of this record being extended seemed very slim. Tottenham were in good form and took the lead after 37 minutes through Jermaine Jenas.

However, Theo Walcott epitomised Arsenal's growing dominance when he rose to the occasion and banged the ball home in the 78th minute. This levelled the tie on the night and guaranteed an intriguing second-leg at White Hart Lane. The Gunners were aware they would have to improve on this performance to make it to the Final.

Away v Tottenham Hotspur

This was a night that everyone at Arsenal will be keen to forget. Jenas gave the home side an early lead after three minutes with a long-range shot. Things went from bad to worse for the visitors and by the time Adebayor netted on 70 minutes, Tottenham had already scored three more times, making the Togolese man's goal little more than a consolation.

In injury time Steed Malbranque completed Tottenham's rout, and with it Arsenal's humiliation. It was a distressing evening, but it should not be allowed to cloud another fine campaign in which Arsène Wenger showed once more that the future for Arsenal is bright indeed.

25 September 2007 Arsenal 2-0 Newcastle United (Bendtner 83, Denilson 89)

31 October 2007 Sheffield United 0-3 Arsenal (Eduardo 8, 50, Denilson 69)

18 December 2007 Blackburn Rovers 2-3 Arsenal (Diaby 6, Eduardo 29, 105)

9 January 2008 Arsenal 1-1 Tottenham Hotspur (Walcott 78)

22 January 2008 Tottenham Hotspur 5-1 Arsenal (Adebayor 70)

ARSENAL TV

Arsenal TV puts fans at the heart of the Emirates, with news, interviews and live action from the Gunners. But what is life like behind the scenes? Channel Editor Daniel Hart puts us in the picture...

There's already lots of football on television, what is special about ArsenalTV?

Arsenal TV as the very title suggests is a channel completely focused on Arsenal FC. Nowhere else will a fan be able to watch every minute of first team action. The channel also broadcasts all reserve matches live, and covers all pre-season matches. The channel's build-up shows offer in depth analysis and behind the scenes exclusive interviews and access, plus the opportunity for supporters to air their views on the club in our Fans Forum show presented by popular radio host and all-round Arsenal nut Tom Watt.

What other shows and features do you broadcast?

We also have programmes highlighting the Ladies and Youth sides enabling viewers to be completely up to date with all the club's teams. Apart from the football action we offer several programme strands including a chat show with Bob Wilson. The legendary goalkeeper and broadcaster interviews players from the club's past in incredibly frank interviews. We also have a legends programme and a celebrity fans show, a 'Where Are They Now?' show again presented by Tom Watt, plus regular first-team player features in a show entitled Spotlight. Coupled with these programmes the channel regularly features classic Arsenal matches.

Can you describe a typical working day for you?

My job essentially involves being across all the channel's content, which typically entails arranging the channel's staff, ensuring they are kept busy fulfilling the various programme requirements. I also produce the channel's live output, assessing what content will be included and the stories we'll be concentrating on, and dealing with any technical requirements we have to get the programmes to air.

What has been the funniest, or most memorable, behind-the-scenes moment on ArsenalTV?

The most memorable moment in terms of horror occurred on the launch night when another television company working at the stadium pulled one of our camera cables as we were just about to go to the shot. Five minutes into the channel and we were heading towards an embarrassing disaster. Time seemed to slow for what could only have been a split second as our director went to another camera and the threat was averted as our engineers moved at speed to re-connect us.

However Arsenal TV have an excellent team of people, we work hard but revel in each other's company and laughter is certainly not absent. The antics of Shovell and the way Tom Watt deals with the young callers on Fans Forum have supplied some beautiful on-air moments.

Which Arsenal player that you have yet to interview on ArsenalTV would you most like to feature?

We speak to a member of the first team every week, so the players I would like to appear on the channel the most have to be the stars of yesteryear, particularly Dennis Bergkamp, Ian Wright and Tony Adams. Although any player from the club's past is of obvious interest to the channel, but those three guys would be fantastic and I'm sure the fans would love them to appear on one or any of our programmes.

Arsenal On The Road

ARSENAL ON THE ROAD

Across the four competitions they were involved in, Arsenal played in cities up and down the country – and across the continent of Europe. Here, we plot across a map of England and the rest of Europe the progress of Arsenal's travels throughout 2007/08.

28 October
Liverpool
D 1-1

19 August
Blackburn
Rovers D 1-1

29 December
Everton
W 4-1

8 April
Liverpool
L 4-2

31 October
Sheffield
United W 3

18 December
Blackburn
Rovers
W 3-2(aet)

6 January
Burnley
W 2-0

28 April
Derby
County
W 6-2

9 March
Wigan
Athletic
D 0-0

29 March
Bolton
Wanderers
W 3-2

16 February
Manchester
United L 4-0

2 February
Manchester
City W 3-1

13 April
Manchester
United L 2-1

11 May
Sunderland
W 1-0

23 February
Birmingham
City D 2-2

23 February
Birmingham
City D 2-2

12 November
Reading
W 3-1

1 December
Aston Villa
W 2-1

26 December
Portsmouth
D 0-0

19 January
Fulham
W 3-0

22 January
Tottenham
Hotspur
L 5-1

23 March
Chelsea
L 2-1

15 September
Tottenham
Hotspur
W 3-1

29 September
West Ham
W 1-0

Arsenal On The Road

FA CUP
CHAMPIONS LEAGUE
PREMIERSHIP
CARLING CUP
5 December Newcastle United D 1-1
9 December Middlesbrough L 2-1
15 August Sparta Prague W 2-0
7 November Slavia Prague D 0-0
2 October Steuau Bucharest W 1-0
4 March AC Milan W 2-0
27 November Sevilla L 3-1
Arsenal
ELLISON'S

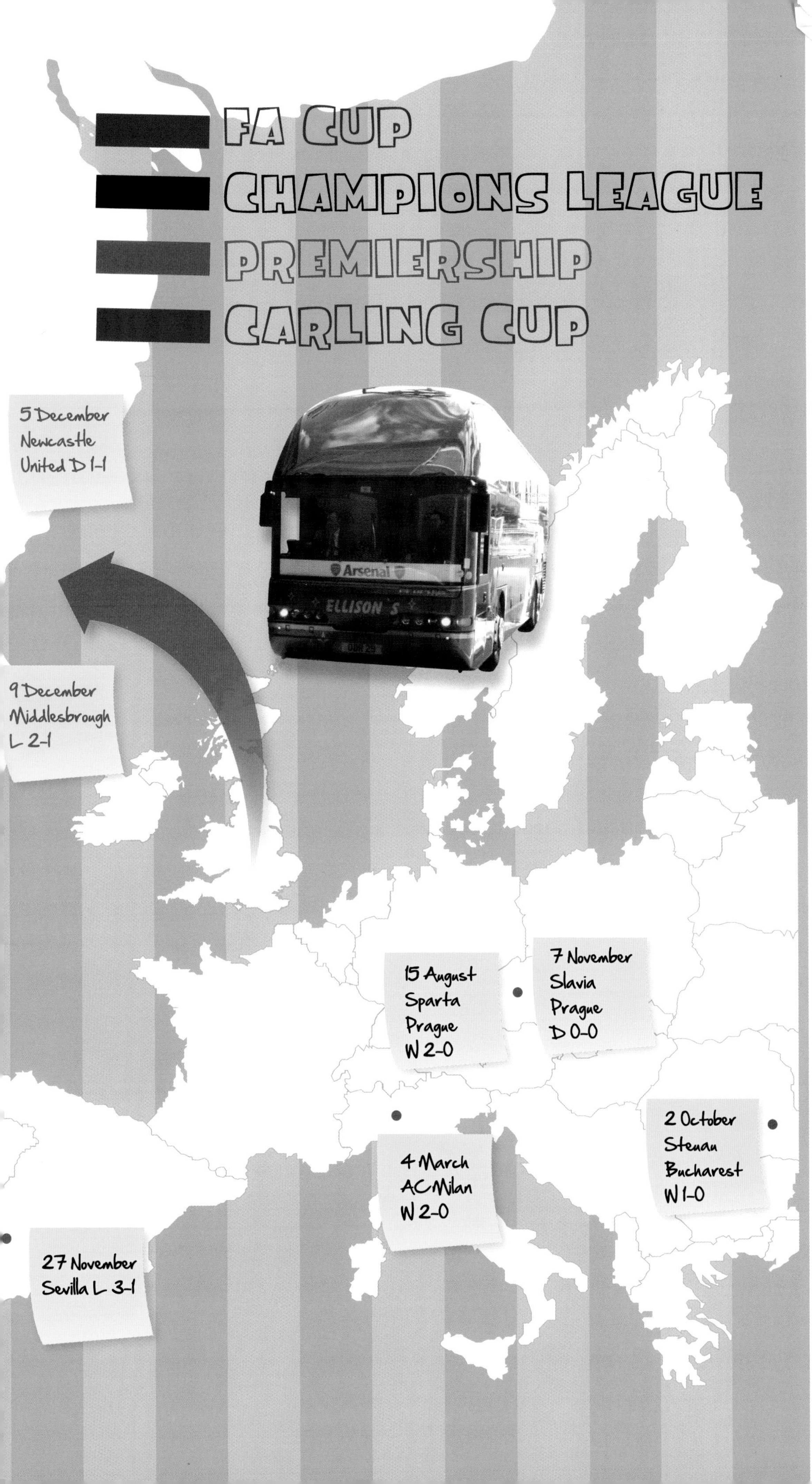

STRIKING GOLD!

Meet Arsenal's main strikers – and stand well back for these guys are seriously deadly shooters. One was born in Africa, one in Brazil, one in Holland and one in England – but all four are regularly on fire in front of goal...

EMMANUEL ADEBAYOR

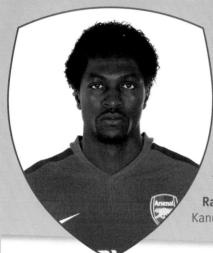

Date of birth: February 26, 1984

Previous Clubs: Metz, Monaco

The knowledge: The top scorer for 2007/08, Emmanuel continues to go from strength to strength. The man who says he likes to "treat the ball as though it is something special" has become something special himself in the eyes of Gunners fans. His height, pace and power make him a dangerous opponent. He scores in big games and also notches hat-tricks, including two against Derby County last season. Mr Wenger says there is more to come from 'Manu'. What an exciting thought!

Random fact: Emmanuel's hero is former Gunners striker Nwankwo Kanu. He even shares the same shirt number - 25!

NICKLAS BENDTNER

Date of birth: January 16, 1988

Previous Club: FC Copenhagen

The knowledge: Strong, tall and powerful, Nicklas is a traditional centre-forward with a modern twist. As well as being formidable in the air, and a fantastic leader of the line, he also has the skill of a support striker. Little wonder that he is valued so highly by supporters! He can also be an explosive substitute, which he showed when he scored with his first touch having been sent on against Tottenham. True class.

Random Fact: Nicklas was voted Danish Talent of the Year for 2007.

EDUARDO

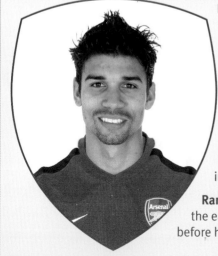

Date of birth: February 25, 1983

Previous Clubs: CBF Nova Kennedy, Bangu Atletico Clube, Inter Zapresic, Dinamo Zagreb

The knowledge: No wonder Arsène Wenger was so keen to land the services of the Croatian: he scored 73 goals in 104 appearances for Dinamo Zagreb. Eduardo was showing every sign of amassing an impressive scoring rate for the Gunners too, before a broken leg curtailed his first season in the Premiership. Prior to this he had proved to be a very handy striker, who could score all manner of different strikes: from distance, close-range and with head or foot. His return from injury is eagerly awaited.

Random Fact: Eduardo was born in Rio De Janiero, Brazil and – as the eagle-eyed of you might have noted – was born a year and a day before his strike partner Adebayor.

ROBIN VAN PERSIE

Date of birth: August 6, 1983

Previous club: Feyenoord

The knowledge: Robin first burst into the nation's consciousness when he scored twice for Arsenal in the 2005 FA Cup semi-final against Blackburn Rovers. He has since become one of Europe's most feared strikers, thanks to his winning combination of skill in the build-up and a powerful, accurate shot. His recent injuries have robbed Arsenal of his services for lengthy periods, but he continues to bounce back in style and with fierce determination to terrorise more defences.

Random fact: Robin's nicknames are Percy and RVP.

CARLOS VELA

Date of birth: March 1, 1989

Previous Clubs: Guadalajara, Osasuna, Celta Vigo

The knowledge: Nippy Mexican Carlos shot to prominence in 2005 when he helped Mexico win the FIFA U-17 World Championships, top scoring with five goals in the tournament to win the Golden Boot. It was Mexico's first world title at any level. After joining Arsenal in 2007, he completed a successful season-long loan with Osasuna in Spain and has now been allocated the No 12 shirt at Arsenal. He is ready to take the Premiership by storm!

Random Fact: Carlos' older brother Alejandro plays for Mexican top flight side Jaguares de Chiapas.

THEO WALCOTT

Date of birth: March 16, 1989

Previous Club: Southampton

The knowledge: Before he even kicked a ball for Arsenal, Walcott had already been to a World Cup Final tournament. He had been awarded a reputation as an exceptional prospect and he has gone on to prove this perception to be true. Initially used as a "super sub" he showed he could turn games with his pace and tricks. He has since become a more regular starter, and his brace of goals against Slavia Prague and Birmingham City suggest he could amass quite a scoring record for the Gunners.

Random fact: Theo once appeared on All-Star Mr & Mrs on ITV with his girlfriend Melanie Slade.

WHICH GUNNER ARE YOU?

All Arsenal fans idolise the players and dream of the day when they can represent their favourite Club. But have you ever thought which Gunners star you most closely resemble? Take this quiz and find out if you're a defensive dynamo, a midfield maestro or a hot-shot striker. Keep a tally of which answers you choose, and then discover at the bottom of the opposite page which Gunner you are. Enjoy!

1 **In football, do you consider the touchline to be:**

a) That line that you boot the ball towards when you're eliminating danger in your own penalty area.

b) A part of the pitch you rarely see – you like to do your business in the middle of the park.

c) A line that you skim up and down at pace, with the ball at your feet.

2 **When you want to greet someone, do you say:**

a) Bonjour!

b) Ola!

c) Hello!

3 **How many different haircuts have you had in the past three years?**

a) Just the one, really. I don't like to mess about with my hair much.

b) Two or three, my hair always looks supercool!

c) I slightly tweaked it about six months ago, but it's stayed much the same really.

4 **If your best friend challenged you to a sprint race in your local park, would you:**

a) Come first, because you're fast and enthusiastic.

b) Win, because you're a born winner.

c) Have completed the race before your friend had even started.

5 What would make you do a cartwheel in the air?
a) Anything, I love to jump and flip!
b) Scoring a goal, something I've been doing a lot more of lately.
c) I prefer the aeroplane celebration, myself.

6 On an ideal day, are goals there to be:
a) Stopped.
b) Created.
c) Scored.

Answers

Mostly As: You are Kolo Toure. You're as solid as a rock, enthusiastic and enjoy elaborate celebrations. You'd be a star in any football team's back four!

Mostly Bs: You are Cesc Fabregas. You are at your happiest in the middle of the park, with a brand new haircut to compliment your silky football skills.

Mostly Cs: You are Theo Walcott. You're a fast and talented striker, with a touch of the old-fashioned Englishman about you.

junior GUNNERS

It has been another fantastic year for the coolest supporters club in the Premiership. So why not let club mascot Gunnersaurus show you through just some of the main highlights?

JUNIOR GUNNERS FORUM

This was attended by Manuel Almunia and Gael Clichy and was held in the Press Conference room at Emirates Stadium. 100 lucky Junior Gunners members were invited to the event. They quizzed Manuel and Gael about topics as diverse as football, cars, movies and even girlfriends. Manuel said: "It was funny because we're used to being asked questions about football, but they asked us questions about our lives. It was different, it was interesting." Gael added: "It was really funny and good for the kids. Without them, we are nothing so we have to give in order to receive."

GET WELL, EDUARDO!

Prior to the clash with Middlesbrough, matchday mascot Peter presented the recently-injured Eduardo with a collection of 'Get Well' cards from Junior Gunners members. He also presented the Croatian beautifully-bound book containing 500 messages from well-wishers around the world.

ALSO

Another successful Members Day was held at Emirates Stadium. Lucky Junior Gunners members got to watch the first-team squad being put through its paces by manager Arsène Wenger in a special training session.

The Junior Gunners department is now accepting nominations for deserving members of our young supporters club. There is a variety of different categories to nominate a member of your family or a friend who is a truly unique Junior Gunner.

BECOME A JUNIOR GUNNER AND BECOME ARSENAL'S MOST IMPORTANT SIGNING!

You will earn:

- The chance to become a team mascot!
- The opportunity to come to the Junior Gunners Christmas party!
- The chance to play on the Emirates Stadium pitch!
- The chance to join the Arsenal ballboy/ballgirl squad!
- The chance to ask the players a question at the Junior Gunners forum!
- The opportunity to pick up a Junior Gunners award from a player!
- Access to discounted match tickets (subject to availability)!

Plus much more including...

- A fantastic Junior Gunners membership pack including an Arsenal beanie hat to show your colours and a zip-up pencil case filled with fantastic Arsenal stationery!
- Exclusive competitions and events
- Exclusive Junior Gunners newsletter 3 times a season and much, much more...

All for just £22 per season.*

* £20 when joining the Direct Debit scheme, £27 Republic of Ireland, Europe and the rest the world.

TOP 10 GOALS

There's no better sight in football than the ball bulging the back of the net. Be it a long-range piledriver, a rising volley or a smashing header – they all catch the eye. So sit back and enjoy our selection of the Top 10 goals of the season. Pick that one out!

 Abou Diaby v Derby County (h)
September 22, 2007

This was a nice long-range howitzer of a strike. The Frenchman picked up a loose ball, danced round a few defenders and fired an unstoppable shot into the top corner of the goal. Pick that one out!

 Emmanuel Adebayor v Tottenham Hotspur (a)
September 15, 2007

Having gone behind in the 15th minute, the Gunners had fought back to lead 2-1. Then in the final minute, Adebayor teed himself up to send a glorious volley over Paul Robinson and into the net.

 Theo Walcott v Derby County (a)
April 28, 2008

On a night when a massive eight goals were scored, this one was particularly memorable. The young hot-shot sailed into the opponent's penalty area, evaded his marker in style and then curled a fantastic shot into the far corner of the net. Glorious.

 Eduardo v Sheffield United (a)
October 31, 2007

Song passed to Bendtner, who in turn slid the ball to Eduardo on the edge of the penalty area. The Croatian quickly fired the ball into the top corner. It was the third goal of his Arsenal career, and a memorable one at that!

 Cesc Fabregas v Slavia Prague (h)
October 23, 2007

Just five minutes into this tie, Alexander Hleb bamboozled a chain of defenders, then looked up and sent a surgically-precise pass to Fabregas. Inside the area, the midfield ace curled home a glorious shot which bulged the net.

 Emmanuel Adebayor v Reading (a)
November 12, 2007

This was a slickly built team goal. In the 51st minute, Tomas Rosicky cut the ball back from the left to Fabregas. The Spaniard knocked the ball to Adebayor who was able to nonchalantly sidefoot the ball into the corner of the net.

⚽ **Denilson v Newcastle United (h) September 25 2007**

Abou Diaby claims the assist for this goal, Denilson was the scorer and all who watched it can consider themselves lucky. In the dying seconds of the game, the Frenchman fed the Brazilian who powered home a belter into the top corner of the net.

STAT ATTACK!

League Table	P	W	D	L	F	A	GD	Pts
1 Man Utd	38	27	6	5	80	22	58	87
2 Chelsea	38	25	10	3	65	26	39	85
3 Arsenal	38	24	11	3	74	31	43	83

Arsenal.com player of the year: Cesc Fabregas

Most appearances: Gael Clichy (48 +1 sub)

Top goalscorer: Emmanuel Adebayor (30)

⚽ **Nicklas Bendtner v Tottenham Hotspur (h) December 22, 2007**

With 15 minutes to go of this North London derby, young Bendtner rose from the bench. With his first touch of the game, he scored the winner with a powerful header. What a way to arrive!

⚽ **William Gallas v Chelsea (h) December 16, 2007**

This was a thumping captain's goal. In first-half injury-time Petr Cech missed a left-wing corner from Fabregas and skipper Gallas rose to head home. It was the winning goal and came against the captain's former club. True class.

⚽ **Emmanuel Adebayor v Liverpool (a) April 8, 2008**

With seven minutes left of this pulsating Champions League tie, collecting the ball deep inside his own half, Walcott skipped past tackle after tackle before squaring for Adebayor to tap past Liverpool's Reina. The finish was simple, but the build-up exquisite.

KNOW YOUR CLUB!

THE MANAGER

⚽ Arsène Wenger was born in Strasbourg: true or false?

⚽ Mr Wenger managed Nancy and which other French side?

⚽ Which year did the Frenchman join Arsenal? 1998 or 1996?

⚽ The FA Cup and which other trophy did Wenger win in his first full season with the Gunners?

⚽ True or false: Emmanuel Petit was the first player Wenger bought for Arsenal?

⚽ Wenger won the Double in 1998 and which other year?

⚽ True or false: Mr Wenger has presided over more Arsenal matches than any other Gunners boss?

⚽ Arsène was named Manager of the Year in 1998, 2002 and which other year?

⚽ Did Mr Wenger previously coach in China or Japan?

⚽ Mr Wenger was the first non-British manager to win the Double in England: true or false?

EMIRATES STADIUM

⚽ The first match at Emirates was the testimonial of an Arsenal legend. Who?

⚽ Which rock singer was the first to perform a concert at Emirates Stadium: Bruce Springsteen or Bryan May?

⚽ Which reality television show held auditions at Emirates?

⚽ Who contested the first international fixture to be staged at Emirates?

⚽ What was the total cost of building the Stadium?

⚽ Which year did Emirates Stadium open?

⚽ What is the capacity of the Stadium?

⚽ How many catering points are there in the Stadium: 25 or 250?

⚽ Who were Arsenal's first Premiership opponents at Emirates: Aston Villa or Fulham?

⚽ Who scored Arsenal's first Premiership goal at Emirates?

UEFA CHAMPIONS LEAGUE

- Which team did Arsenal beat 7-0 in October 2007?
- In Arsenal's quarter-final tie at Liverpool in 2008, Abou Diaby and which other Gunner scored?
- In which year did Arsenal reach their first Champions League final?
- And who were their opponents that night?
- Which Gunner scored in that final?
- How many consecutive clean sheets did Arsenal keep in their 2005/06 Champions League campaign?
- Which Italian giants did Cesc Fabregas open the scoring against in March 2008?
- What was the score in the first-leg of Arsenal's quarter-final against Liverpool in April 2008? 1-1 or 2-2?
- In which city was the 2006 Champions League final held?
- Who did the Gunners beat in their Champions League qualifying matches in August 2007? Sparta Prague or Celtic?

PLAYER PROFILES

- What nationality is Emmanuel Adebayor?
- Which country was Tomas Rosicky born in?
- Which club did Robin van Persie join Arsenal from?
- Which city was Justin Hoyte born in: London or Cardiff?
- Is Cesc Fabregas Spanish or German?
- Kolo Toure plays for which international side?
- With which club did Theo Walcott begin his career?
- Did William Gallas win the Premiership at Chelsea?
- Which is Gael Clichy's normal position: left-back or centre-back?
- What nationality is Abou Diaby?

CLUB HISTORY

- Arsenal won their first Double in which year: 1971 or 1973?
- Who did Arsenal beat in the 1994 European Cup Winners' Cup Final: Parma or Plymouth Argyle?
- Which other London club did Arsenal legend Liam Brady once play for?
- Who did Arsenal beat in the 2005 FA Cup Final?
- Which team did the Gunners beat in both domestic cup finals in 1993?
- How long did Arsenal spend at Highbury: 93 years or 103 years?
- In what year did the legendary Dennis Bergkamp join the Club?
- True or false: Arsenal won the league championship in 1992
- In what year did the Club win its first league championship?
- And in which year did the Club win its first FA Cup?

Answers on p61

SPOT THE DIFFERENCE

Can you spot the 9 differences between the two photographs?
Answers on p61

SPOT THE BALL

Where do you think the ball is? – A, B, C, or D?

Answers on p61

GUESS THE GUNNER

We've fuzzed these photographs of Arsenal stars. Can you guess who the three players are? We've added clues to make it easier.

Answers on p61

Clue: He reigns in Spain... and North London

Clue: He's a Dane-namic striker

Clue: This defender can really Coast!

CROSSWORD

Crossword clues

Across

2 Van Persie is this, and so was Dennis! (5)

6 You'll never win a game without at least one of these (4)

7 Arsenal beat Italian giants AC Milan at the San... (4)

10 The first name of our Swiss centre-back star (8)

12 He's our rising Brazilian star (8)

14 Class defender, Mr Sagna (6)

16 The Club's nickname (7)

17 They won Euro 2008 (5)

18 The first Englishman to score at the Emirates, Justin.... (5)

19 The legendary half-back (6)

20 It's the Club home! (9)

Down

1 Arsenal love to collect these (9)

3 Our brilliant Assistant Manager, Pat.... (4)

4 Thierry's old number...and Theo's new one (8)

5 He is the Junior Gunners mascot (12)

8 The surname of Ace Abou.... (5)

9 The goal that is scored from the spot (7)

11 New star Samir Nasri joined from this club (9)

13 Arsenal won this in 1971, 1998 and 2002 (6)

15 The Club's former home (8)

Answers on p61

WORDSEARCH

K	F	X	Y	M	C	E	S	C
R	Z	Q	N	Q	E	B	A	D
O	K	H	C	B	Y	I	G	I
Y	T	A	O	L	N	C	N	A
A	R	U	N	U	I	E	O	B
B	E	R	M	G	R	C	S	Y
E	R	L	N	U	A	T	H	M
D	A	N	O	L	N	S	N	Y
A	H	T	S	A	L	L	A	G

Everyone who plays for Arsenal can pick out a team-mate on a crowded pitch. But do you have the same vision? See if you can find the names of 10 Arsenal players which are hidden in this wordsearch? Good luck!

Here are the names to look for:
Adebayor, Almunia, Cesc, Clichy, Diaby, Eboue, Gallas, Sagna, Song, Toure.

Answers on p61

It was another exciting season for Arsenal in 2007/08. Can they do even better in 2008/09? Keep track of everything here and compare the two campaigns!

FA PREMIERSHIP	SEASON 2007/08	SEASON 2008/09
Final position	Third	
First home win	Fulham 2-1	
First away win	Tottenham 3-1	
First home draw	Manchester United 2-2	
First away draw	Blackburn Rovers 1-1	
First home defeat	None	
First away defeat	Middlesbrough 2-1	

DOMESTIC CUPS	SEASON 2007/08	SEASON 2008/09
FA Cup	Round 5: Manchester United	
Carling Cup	Semi-final: Tottenham Hotspur	

CHAMPIONS LEAGUE	SEASON 2007/08	SEASON 2008/09
Progress	Quarter-final Liverpool	
First home win	Sparta Prague 3-0	
First away win	Sparta Prague 2-0	
First home draw	AC Milan 0-0	
First away draw	Slavia Prague 0-0	
First home defeat	None	
First away defeat	Sevilla 1-3	

GOALS	SEASON 2007/08	SEASON 2008/09
First in Premiership	Van Persie v Fulham	
First in FA Cup	Eduardo v Burnley	
First in Carling Cup	Bendtner v Newcastle United	

TRIVIA QUIZ

PAGE 52/53

True	Sol Campbell
AS Monaco	10
1996	AC Milan
The Premiership	1-1
False	Paris
2002	Sparta Prague
True	
2004	Togolese
Japan	Czech Republic
True	Feyenoord
	London
Dennis Bergkamp	Spanish
Bruce Springsteen	Ivory Coast
The X Factor	Southampton
Brazil and Argentina	Yes
£390 million	Left-back
2006	French
60,000	
250	1971
Aston Villa	Parma
Gilberto	West Ham United
	Manchester United
	Sheffield Wednesday
Slavia Prague	93 years
Emmanuel Adebayor	1995
2006	False: it was 1991
Barcelona	1931
	1930

SPOT THE DIFFERENCE

PAGE 54

SPOT THE BALL   PAGE 55

GUESS THE GUNNER

PAGE 55

A: Cesc Fabregas

B: Nicklas Bendtner

C: Kolo Toure

CROSSWORD

PAGE 56

Across		Down	
2	Dutch	1	Victories
6	Goal	3	Rice
7	Siro	4	Fourteen
10	Philippe	5	Gunnersaurus
12	Denilson	8	Diaby
14	Bacary	9	Penalty
16	Gunners	11	Marseille
17	Spain	13	Double
18	Hoyte	15	Highbury
19	Clichy		
20	Emirates		

WORDSEARCH

PAGE 57

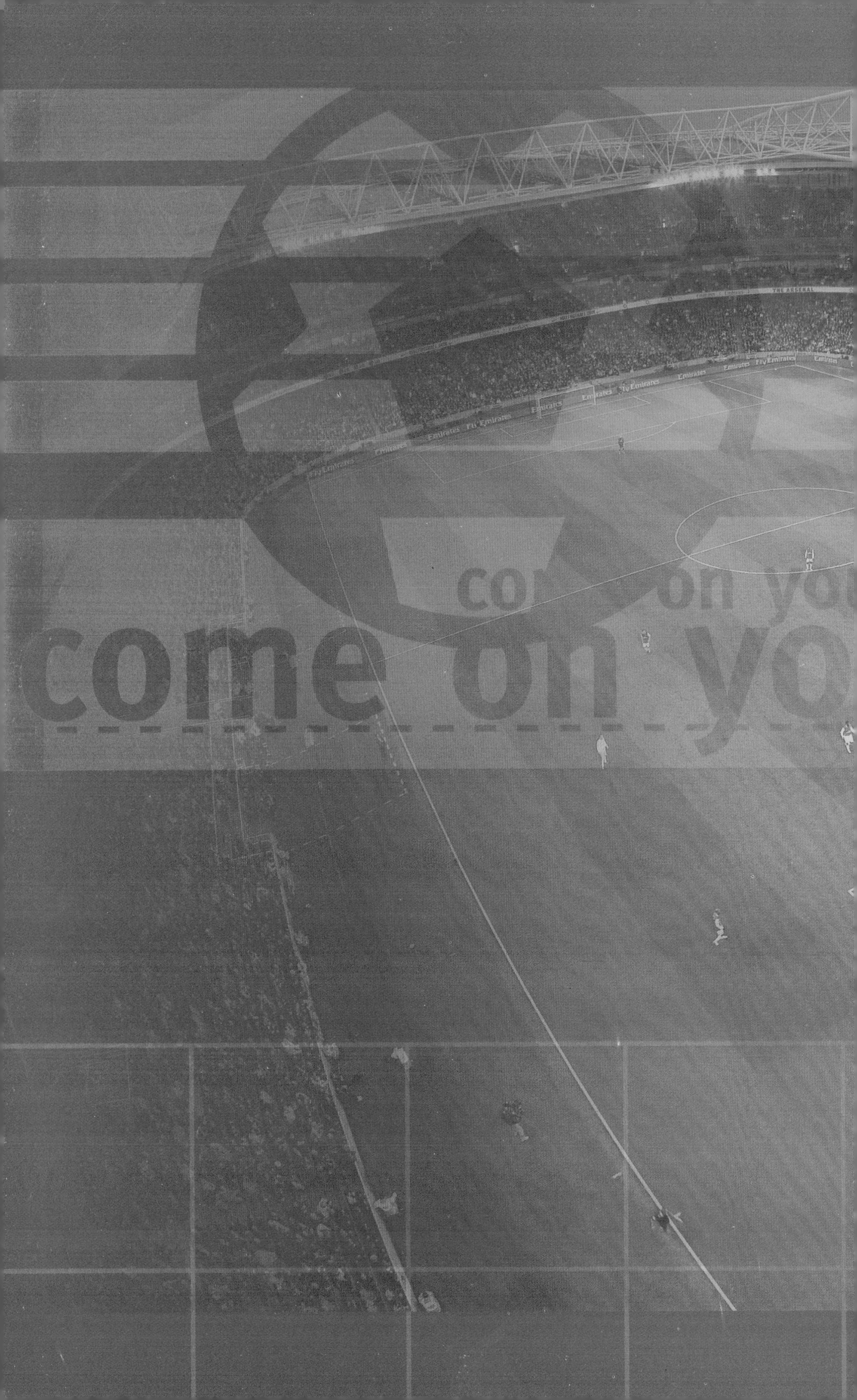
come on yo